The Memoir Blossom

Everyone has a story to tell life from a boy's perspective

-Table of Contents-

Introduction

Acknowledgments

By: Mark G. Wadley

Introduction

Creating your life's journey is the first spark of igniting your Will of Fire. The down falls and up rises we encounter in life are the pen and pencil that writes our life story in history. Your dreams and goals is the bond that seals your legacy. The purpose of producing the Memoir Blossom is to reconstruct the minds of those who believe a dream isn't possible, and motivate those who Will of Fire hasn't been sparked into the journey ahead. Introducing the path of God to people who don't know that he seeks their salvation, and maintaining the words of scripture within any congregation. Believing in the share will of a true apostle for guidance and unwrapping the reality of integrity. Identifying how love and hope fade before my eyes, my community is tearing itself apart and violence has become an aspect of sports and games.

The tears and bones of broken spirits needs the attention of medical aids and health patches. I continue to experiment with different theories and opinions on how to unravel the secrets of the world through my own observations, but the trials and turning points in my life are in full affect. Providing the essential idea and dedication of possible goals and rising above all failures will become the start of ambitious scholars of the future. I believe reaching out to the youth generation and giving them the chance to witness other experiences and soaking the consideration of others, who endured the challenges of life as a tool to shape the youth generation into achievers. I believe that the love of every individual who believes in the faith of dreams and wisdom will become the trophies of success, and the root that holds up the pillar will be the burning spark that motivates all youth among society to become the inspiration for the next generation.

Bold and Gallant

Poem by: M.G. Wadley

Wash away the waters where champions dance, sleep within the mist of the vertical proportions where the victors stands and the fault line meet.

Sunset on wood silk butter, as I shine the armor that's passed down through the bold and gallant.

Wise free engagement, warmth of the kettle that stays lit pass dawn until the pyramids of Egypt reconstruct. Find the plants and vines, strain the venom from the honey oil of our divine nature.

Scales from the dragon's belly, fire of black flames ember crest plate, phoenix flower blooms boom, all white hills among the tune.

Look off into center piece that shines from the belly of the beast of the beauty, please feed the faces of vision. As I look unto my brothers I see the love of what a real brother and friend stand for.

Brother oh friend I love thee amount times ten. Carry the ghost of Mandela, become the spirit of Harriet but the freedom of Turner sparks the rebellion out of oppression.

Places of witches which lie within the labyrinth, between soldier's march among hollow grounds, catacombs of skulls and gold. The Bold champion plunges the demons and monsters that dwells within.

Home of comfort, grapes and oranges juices from a valley between triple mountains on the river path to Michael. People of bronze, natural essences of beauty from the divine. Soaring, floating among the old faces that labored beyond the walls of foundation.

Flavors of core hydration and fundamentals, nutrients enhanced, run child, chase the trumpets of champions, within the locked plastic that wraps the bowl we craft.

Protect, oh yes protect, protect of protection within the proceed of product, blame the ones who gives up and allows the city to burn to ashes. Rebirth of congress, hold onto the lessons of love that dwells among the leaves.

I stand and fight for those who does not have the courage to face the fight in between the shadow of themselves. I stand and fight for the people who has no chances to depict a vision.

Honor the knights armor that has been passed down unto you, many has shed blood and deceived the righteous to continue to survive, remember those who remember you.

They come in many, they come in numbers, but dare shall I never stumble again in front of my loved ones, won't ever close an eye to bare a tear, for I shall prevail and never swear. Beware, foresee and then decide, embark, learn within and apply, for you will win.

Visualize in Abundance

Acknowledgments

As a start, the names that will be read in between the lines plays a significant role on how I made my decisions to pursue my goals and success. From home to school, from school to work, the relationship of family and the genuine consideration of coworkers and childhood friends from the neighborhood. Themes and life lessons from the down falls of martyrs and personal beliefs. Leaders and champions who fought to rise above all misery and negative priorities that will unbalance success. Knowing and understanding the elements of failure the dim glare between the eyes when you know you're done for good. I thank God for placing the papers

that justifies the movement that's
invested within me, my vessel that he has
built and blessed, the knowledge that
manufacturers on how the world goes
around. Opening the closets of love and
to live my life as a passionate man,
appreciating the virtue and independence
that I have read from the words of
divinity. Looking for heaven while hell on
earth, each day I wake up the eye of God
takes a sneak peek through my window.
The beauties of Gods kingdom tip toes
across the wooden planks along my bed
room door. I'm grateful to know there Is a
way to reach Jacobs ladder. I Thank God
for the life you chose for me, my family,
my friends, fear, all the life lessons the
heartbreaks, the failures and
embarrassments. I thank you for your
mercy and blessings, I thank you for the

opportunity of life, truth fully I'm grateful not only as an honorable man but a humble servant. Thank you my heavenly father, Amen.

I kind had to throw in the towel and washed my hands of all dirty business that stained. I realized the mother that raised me and shaped into the gallant champion that words will be remembered in all the fame if history, all aspirations that will live on through my family tree. My Aunt, who was willing to sacrifice her boundaries of success into four children who she personally wanted to save from damnation. Breaking barriers for another life, rebuking bad habits, battling the devils that knock at each door. A true queen that's willing to go through the tides of quick sand, toe to toe with Goliath to keep her kingdom standing strong. I grew up endorsing selfish intentions to keep her love to myself, afraid to let it diffuse to others of the world. A hug with the touch of the softest fabric, and woven by the artisans of paradise. Teaching and guiding me from a boy to a man. Training my mind and body to endure the pressures of the world. Entrusting me with blessings she never received, pushing me to take my family and life beyond the stars of astrology. I thank you Aunt Angie me from a boy to a man. Training my mind and body to endure the pressures of the world. Entrusting me with blessings she never received, pushing me to take my family and life beyond the stars of astrology. I thank you Aunt Angie for hearing my cries and concealing my pain even before it surfaced. I'm grateful to have you as my mother and inspiration, I couldn't be blessed with anything better. I'm glad to have my uncle in my life, I'm proud to have what other people are not able to feel or see the labor of what a true man stands for. Laying out the blue print that gives everything a loving home offers, all the abundance that keeps the connection strong. Uncle Larry I thank you for standing firm as a role model and the family man that every man needs to be. Thank my Uncle Larry for everything. I would like to acknowledge my friends and coworkers for all your support, I would like to honor all icons and inspirations who has passed down their legacy into the arms of a winner. I want thank any man or women who hasn't given up on the adventure that stands before thee. I thank you for standing strong, thank you for your courage and admiration, truth fully I'm grateful.

As the moon whistles

Poem by: M.G. Wadley

Grey scales and wine ponds, stones of

pillar dust, as I travel to the earth my

engine on its thrust.

The bobcat smiles on the winter

Solstice the light embarks a great

ordeal of lust. Seniors of age, guru of

wisdom, stars of the sky, junky of gold

drink and white wine

when the moon whistles.

The night has come, jet black aroma,

my feet begins to hide as the moon

peaks behind the stars, come and

celebrate as the moon whistles.

Visualize in Abundance

Chapter 1

The light within

In life, we only see what we think we can change, or assume we can make a difference. People of our nation are blinded with hatred and envy towards their brothers and sisters, they seem to struggle with their achievements or dreams. As one group of people we can overcome our struggles through love and peace, also with enthusiasm so we can have an impact on history. Our lives and future are determined by the choices we make, and the actions we take to get there. In our generation, today the youth civilization has become confused and overwhelmed with denial, some people lack the academic requirements, and always produces anger and hateful expressions towards people, objects, and the trend of society. From my observation, people who give up on their life because they believe they no purpose or lack motivation. Look beyond the objects that has been offered, look past the ignorance of any dark or insidious phase that you have encountered. If u look back at your regrets and the past mistakes you made and dwell, it will be difficult to move forward towards your next reward. The regrets will become an abstract bolt in your failure and as time goes on, the boat will slowly sink. Let God be the light within, allow God to be your first thought, acknowledge the fruits of your labor as the blessing from the father above, and then the life you truthfully wish to live will no longer be a pigment of your fantasies. Nothing in life is perfect, but have the courage to make your promise guaranteed, stand tall even when u watch your dream crumble. Sometimes you must pick up the crumbs before you can enjoy the entire plate. Foster God's love to always give the next slice, let the love be the light within.

In every household, there is a back bone, the one or two people who keeps the family above float. In my personal belief, every member of the house is the back bone for one another. In our nation history, different cultures contributed different attributes and values among society that benefits us today. As a citizen, as a man of God and honor, as a son, as a brother and most of all as my own man who stands tall with the essence of peace among society. You can overcome lies and deception, as the truth swindles from out of the furnace your ambition will be ready to ignite. Embrace your beautiful silhouette, feel the vibe of your aroma, cast it out as the words you speak when you express your dreams. Use the same words that you would in a conversation about success that goes beyond the stars. Love the message that you bring, love the message that you receive, elaborate the meekness of the content, understand the content that sparked the light within. Sometimes I had to allow the light that shine within me diffuse and explore the realms around the hearts of others. Evaluate yourself, make your heart the next boys inspiration, shape your love into the truth. As the little kings and queens that are our daughters and sons from heaven may believe in that pursuit of love. As I continue to walk among the streets of Philadelphia my feet are in the mud and heaven gates are on the whim of truth for my family and legacy. Walking in blind faith, allowing my ears and eyes to be my door way to the faith I believe and the belief of the words that I speak into existence. Sometimes as I look beyond the window as I write I think about the lost souls that were taken, I think about how I refuse to let the streets devour my life and opportunity, I refuse to let the misery of the world adapt within my joy of success. Allowing my memories to be keep my motivation dominant in my rise from the slums. Elaborating on reasons to keep my light shining bright, dipping and dabbing in the different knowledge of God to become a better person.

Even this very day I'm fighting against the devil temptation and ambition to stop my story from being told. The scars, the bruises, the pain, the phases of broken dreams, the very blood you taste when you walk among the gutter. Looking at death each day you walk to the next corner, wondering about the angels that watch over the crown on my head. Thinking about how God will bend the next bullet to spare my life, understanding the pain that will diffuse among my loved ones, watching as tears drop, and the life in the struggle becomes more obsolete. Coming from the poorest parts, where bright lights, working hard through the bumps and lost hope are on the other side of each door.

Each time you turn the knob there it goes, the ups and downs the twist and turns, heaven is a block away but the wars of the field, the battle of surviving the chaos that's archaic in any lane is the risk you should decide to take. Looking at life through the eyes of a poor boy's dream, willing to create the depiction of Jacobs Ladder at the tip of my fingers, the world is in the palm of my hands, and Jesus spirit continue is to walk with me down each dark alley and street corner as I bustle for success. We only human, we all make mistakes, we are only flesh but born to withhold our bodies as temples and Mountains, the feeling of flowing rivers, smiles brighter than Eden itself will be the abundant festivity that will embolden my prosperity.

Never forget who you are because the world surely wont, the world we live in will judge your intuition, and try to breach the very thing you love most. Ask yourself, how badly do you want what you desire, how much dedication are you willing to put in to reach the next level, what are you willing to sacrifice to behold that capacity of influence. I pray to God so that my heart burning flame won't blow out. I pray to God because as I look towards the long run and the path that's within my perception becomes an enigma. I still vow to triumph through the blizzards and storms, the solitude of the ghost that haunts and taunts the oracle of what reality is to you. I ask anyone who reads these words, keep the dignity to honor those whose light and heart isn't on the path to God, change their radiant devotion to the almighty. God speaks through me as I speak unto you, his voice jolts among the ears of my heart, and I deeply accepts his messages and grace. "So, I ask and say unto you, keep the light that shines within you alive, keep the love within as it vegetates keep it conclusive, keep it in the prospect of God."

A Dance Between Lemon and Lime

Poem by: Mark G. Wadley

The sunset sings on wishers bay,
the yellow brim blend, on a
winters day. They thrust and
turn when love evolves, as
we lay the stamp they mail it
off. Skim the surface with the
blade, spin then spin on
wishers bay, the road is long
on a summers day, but we

still chase love through the
spring of May.

Cruising through the life of
multitudes, deflation the sons
of solitudes, the light bulb
shatters as the grey aroma
sparks the scent of lemon and
lime, as humans we skim the
surface from earths
approaches.

Chuckles and buckles, brim and
scent, the dance between
lemon and lime, as we lay
them upon the bin. Cover
and swarm around the scent,

breathe the air of lover's twist. Take to the liquid, mix the spread, swipe it on before you lay to bed. As you look through the window, you come to see, birds and bees, life and heat. There's plenty to eat, enough to feast, fuse the lime with a country beat.

The lemon so sweet but sours the mouth, now its watered down within the drought. Open the box, and unwrap the package and remain *detoxed, conclude the maximum.*

Watch the dance between lemon and lime, squeeze the juices from the core, look how the liquid rains and pour. Now pick up the cup and drink.

Visualize in Abundance

Chapter 2

Complete Nutrition

In every Individual, there are chapters we must write to, or mysteries we must unravel. The world is filled with puzzles and pieces these are the parts we must combine to build that bridge to change. Sometimes as you face the very conflicts you lack personally you start to identify the overall purpose to change and progress. I believe change is the next step in life, and one of the most important components that we use to progress to the next level in life.

People change their environments or society with persuasion or speech, even the personal stand points of life that's on the verge for modification and perfection. Many leaders of our nation had a dream or goal for change, Dr. Martin Luther King Jr dream was to change racial acts within America, giving his all from his heart to his explicit dialogue, his splendid vision of a world that was inspired from God heart. Even Malcom x who died as a Martyr for his beliefs, had to make some type of pigment of change to have that type of impact in history. Reaching out to the brother and sisters that were at spitting image of himself, reaching out to another world while hell on earth, obtaining the power of persuasion, honoring the trust of the people who believes in his word and testimonies. Adam Clayton Powell surged his voice to be heard within social environments such as schools, community meetings. Supporting as an activist of the Civil rights movement, even the legacy and footsteps of his father preaching within the tabernacle of the pulpit. These legacy leaders These icons passed down their legacy so that we can all progress to keep dreams possible. I'm grateful to have Nelson Mandela stand and look past the whips and scars of the broken families of his people. The shattered love, the will to expand his mind even when chains and locks confine his freedom. I Thank you Nelson Mandela I'm appreciative of your courage and your

heroic vision of peace. The new
generation holds the key, and the
aspect of history standing strong, our
history, dreams, and goals lives on
through you and me. Believe the
opportunity you make will bend the
ears of doubters, but protect the
knowledge that is given in all forms.
All around the world there are
dreams, dreams that most people
can't imagine but will soon become
reality. In every journey, you accept
there will be a protagonist, antagonist,
conflict, climax and resolution.
Become the hero of your journey, be
the individual who stands even when
you don't see anything in return, there
may not be a light at the end of the
tunnel or the person you love the most
to greet you with open arms. Look

towards the sun and moon, look beyond space and heaven look within the core of your heart, squeeze out the madness and become superman of the flight you choose to catch. Avoid the thought and mindset of believing that living the life that's crying out in your heart is the choice of a coward. Be who you are and rebel against those who invites the devil to their door step. Block them, keep them from your presence, keep them from your agenda, keep them from what you love the most. Pray to God in your most humble and honorable intent to progress within yourself. Run, keep running on the golden trail that leads you beyond the bounds of the wonderland you seek. Look on high, continue to climb, climb even when your finger tips are bleeding and your mouth is full of mud. Your body is heavy, the climb up is getting steeper but the way back down seems harder than the start. Reach the turning point in your life, decide the nativity while you climb, choose wisely of the stones you pull and the vines you skim. Beware of the teachings from those that sound influential but have false intentions for your success. Beware of those who speak of your success in the manner of support, sometimes it's the same mouth that glorify your ambition that intends to break you down. Know what's genuine and real, realize the truth when you hear it, feel the vibe of the conversation and it will be your personal decision to decide the truth. I found the climax in my story so far when I found the person that was hiding from within, my over view of the women I loved and adored. The people I would allow to represent me, even when I'm not present plays an assertive part on the turning points on my journey to the top. For a long time, I was afraid of the world around me, not the people or the environment I was raised in, but the abstract thought of knowing nothing is promised or guaranteed. I have watched the best of the best slip and buckle, the toughest of the bunch fall into despair, the less fortunate rise above the hell hole they were captive in. Reach it, reach the peak to walk over the meadow that will change the outer box of your legacy. As I continued to wonder and imagine the visual concept of the picture I wanted to paint, the strokes and blushes started to become more settled, the water color will cry and run down the pages. The smiles and brilliant glows of the faces you crave to indulge, the excitement of the women or girl you love, to feel the energy and grasp the heart that you are willing to keep hold forever. Sometimes you must experience the worst and operate among the deceitful obsession. Swerve along the road that you are willing to dedicate and accelerate within a hazard or crash you will continue to encounter. Overall you create your inspiring story, you individually define your destiny, it's your personal choice to choose the high way that will accelerate the hands of time. Eat and crave the fruits of knowledge, take within all the nutrients and protein, shake it up well, inhale some fresh air stretch a muscle or two, tag a friend and bring them along for the ride. Wake up tomorrow, and make a complete change to anything not beneficial, break and stem of violence or the company of misery. Know what you are willing to go through hells fire for and then within due time you will take the extra step to create that bridge to change.

Lessons with no love

Poem by: M.G. Wadley

Queen of the Nile, queen of the kings,

why do you serve the peasants of

royal solitude. Queen of queens, why

do slumber while the servant feasts,

why do you cleanse your feet without

the proper care.

Does the crocodile of the deep

swallows the lamb that has been

slaughtered by the priest, the ox

cuddles outside the synagogues and

the blue jay bathes in honey tea?

Visualize in Abundance

Chapter 3

Fostered Hatred

Hate is nothing more than a desire within an individual, hate can eat you up like poison. It feeds and feeds until it swallows you dominantly, and spits you out like yesterday's garbage. Most hate is ignited within a household or environment depending on their personal condition or situation. Hate has been within our nation and foreign countries for hundreds of years. As a people, we can abolish hate with love, hope and respect. These components are the bridge to eternal peace, in my understandings hatred spreads faster than love because people have their own ambitions and selfish motives to achieve their own goal. Hate can destroy a society or civilization of people. Most people can't see the light because they're blinded by it, but if even the slightest light is visible the brightest light will shine through. So far in my life journey I have seen hate tear families apart, friends, even the connection of brotherly love. I wish hate could vanish from the earth's atmosphere. Even the word itself didn't exist, but it seems as hate itself is too great of a component to take on individually and head on. The idea I have that will reduce the level of hate within my community, would be to turn the little bit of hate that surrounds the sensation of my heart into love. Allowing the love from within me block out the hate that dwells among society, and looking to the father above to cleanse the air that surrounds the crowns of our head. This will be like two raging forest fires cancelling each other out. The idea of reducing and changing hate within the world would be too great, to probably even imagine, but it is possible. I believe to break this regenerating curse, would be to look in the mirror at the person on the other side of the glass, and predict how much love he or she has spread within the world. The Bloodshed and the cries of a girl who life is in shambles her feet are at the bottom of the barrel, and the lid is closed shut. No light, no voices, just the angry girl who feels as though the world owes her. No finances, low income and his or her children wants their wonderland now, but it's the taunting thought to this family who can barely keep bread on the table. Watching the water turn on and off, the summers started to dry out and the water plugs goes from being shut to never opening. Counting down the days of the school year because breakfast, lunch and dinner won't always be prepared on the regular anymore. Awaiting those hot summer days until twelve o clock on the dot to receive our lunch, snack time was at three so staying out of trouble was out of the question. Tired as mule and the night is to come, kids but in the same bracket as men, exposed to the sins of the world around us and forced to comply against our positive intent. Soaking up the sequence of the life that never progresses in any dream, settling for the less cause and ideals from the torn shades and cloths of home.

Observing how envy prospers in the eyes of a killer, personally knowing, and forsaking the skeletons in the attic. "So, I say unto you, study and understand the lifestyle you accept into your world. Understand that accepting the deeds of the unrighteous will subdue the sanity that still has its roots standing strong." Breaking the love of a mother's opportunity to hold her kids, stopping the phase of broken bones and bruises to care and tend too. Don't be the one to live with guilt, don't be the one that sees the ghost from the past and it haunts you until your six to eight feet under. You see, I had to block some demons and devils of my own, learning and adapting on how to release my energies, when and where always played its part on how I cranked the channel but I learned how to manage the way it diffuses. Learn how to forgive and give mercy, as you grow older the loving heart that you secured as a child runs away, it runs off into the fields of the unknown and becomes hostage in a foreign land. Climbing over mountains and hills, encountering beasts that seeks to devour and destroy, broken hearts and promises, hands and feet in shackles but with no one to love. You find the love that ran away but its features and identity has changed, the heart within is broken and cannot be fixed, the glass that surrounds it has been shattered. The warmth that it feeds on turns cold, the flower that was bright grows into a thorn, raped and abused, mistreated and misplaced, now the heart that you once protected stands before you, now what do you see. "So, I say unto you if the man or women that loses the love that's within the ways of the world, seek it and find so that someone can learn of the mass that holds it together. Even if someone chooses to throw it overboard, catch it before it drops, and offer it to the next person who seeks love. If no one has mercy on your life, do not stoop down into the den of the devil and become like them, shove and push them to the side for the kingdom of God has seen your heart." It's hard to convince anyone who reads these words to live by the languages of my heart, but one thing I will say is that it won't be a waste of time to try. Feel the difference in the way you walk and the breaths you take, feel the spirits that will transpire and revolve around your lips as you speak of the fruits from the tree of life into existence. Discard the hate and the aspects of damnation for it will gobble the street lights that keeps your road ignited, do not stray or forsake the beauty of your love because that's all you have. "So, I say unto you, bathe in the waters of heaven and stabilize yourself within its walls, invite the angels that guides you to the father above and keep the blessings of the divine with spirit."

Nightmares in the attic

Poem by: M.G. Wadley

The night has come and the final hour has blocked out the sunshine from the living. Multiple shots as he stumbles across the floor, wine and beer splashes across the counter as he storms out the rear.

The night is cold and muggy, Satan whispers and giggles in my ear while I observe a walking corpse that's soon to be. He turns around and I pull the trigger twice. Bright lights form behind the bushes as he drops to the puddles of the ground. Never again will you hurt another.

Young and beautiful, pretty and proud always creating the bright light of the room. Caring for the animals that surrounds the neighborhood park.

I should have been more easy and gentle with her, and now she's gone. I can only imagine her cries. I can only see the tears as she fears her body losing life. No one to help or support just why wasn't I there to protect her, just why.

It's been a year so far since you've been gone and now I celebrate the *new year with no love from the person I love the most. Cracks and rubble across the marble floor, everything was perfect until I lost everything in a blink of an eye. He did whatever he desired to my lovely flower and I couldn't protect her. Was it because I was a strict father, was it because God knows the truth behind my own revelation. Am I a man who doesn't have the ability to protect his own, how could I be so dumb and stupid, how could I be so blindsided.*

Now days, death is the only thing that will satisfy me, death to anyone who tries to harm or take what's mine, never again will I be an angel in the midst of devils.

The news scourges the television with homicides and murder. Babies cry as the wolves of a full moon swindles the weak in packs dragging out those of a threat or hunger to see light again. Filled with anger and rage, even the funeral has long passed, my justice will be served when I'm satisfied.

The rain drenches my clothes and head as I shovel up the remains of this scum bag. Smiles and giggles, laughter of confidence right before I plunge the casket door open. A faint voice speaks to me from the sweep of the wind, bee is that you, as I stumble in the mud my back hits the ground and butterflies rises from the casket of the man who took my daughter away from me.

Headed home in the storm of the night, clouds form pillars of skulls and black soles, flash backs of the life that no longer exist, just misery of what these hands did in the past. Voices of my flower still haunts the echo of cries that diffuses along the plumbing of the kitchen.

The pipes burst, owls and ravens scattered along the window seat as the water runs cold the air thickens with roses and plums, her aroma naturally springs to life, but it's still my fault she's gone.

Days and nights continues to pass me by, while I sit and think of the only daughter a father could cherish, I guess the world gives back what is given. I look unto the father above to have mercy on my spirit and love in the next life. Only if I didn't take that girls life that day, maybe mine will still be collecting butterflies.

Visualize in Abundance

Chapter 4

Dreams and Hope

Can a child dream farther than they can see, or is the real question can a child dream a dream that they can see in their future? As I continue to grow goals started to become fairytales and hoop dreams growing up in North Philly, the boys and girls who look like me just let their dreams be flushed away. Rinsing down the hope that once upheld the beams and scales that we use as a craving for support, this use to be the undecided attachment for success. Some people dream end when they hit their freshman year of high school and their goals are nothing but an empty box. First it starts by a lack of focus and interest, then here comes the tired eyes and excuses not to show anymore. Now it's the in between series of reasons, maybe it's child on the way and there are no other options to rely on, maybe there is a family issue or emergency that forces your plans to twist for the better. Truthfully, I don't know the truth of anyone life or tribulations that they have stood up against. If there is not any faults or flaws to why you will need to throw out the hope you have cared for, do not let your blessings be in vain. "So, I say unto you anyone who truthfully seeks the positive deeds of their labor, God shall wash your hands to handle your dirty work, remember with just a speck of light your frowns can turn to smiles, your tears can cease and part, and the frowns of giving up is flipped upside down if you just believe." In history, the past inspirations who has contributed to the development of our opportunities today have left us the torch of hope so that the pigment of hope we crave does not dry out. In my generation, the youth are the new icon and inspiration to any child who believes a dream is possible. These flash mobs and gangs of today are way too relevant in the lives of these corrupted teens, from my point of view violence has become the spark of hope, but the dream itself vanishes into the wilderness because of the trials and road blocks that come into play. Leaving behind the trails of ignorance and deception will flow down the creek until the baby in   the basket finds it useful. I believe the young men and women of my generation are lazy and afraid of their own power and knowledge. Knowing you can change the world is one of the highest distinguished honors you can achieve, so don't waste it and toss it to the side. The power and knowledge to me isn't in the money or any aspect that values a great ordeal of lust, the power that I believe in is having the ability to change the perspective and thought process of another person about life. Also, providing a motivational drive that will run with them on that path that will open up doors to success. Dreams and hope are the components that keeps our thought process on the rise and the hope that we keep sacred is the key that keeps the idea of our imagination possible.

A Breeze Beyond Her Beauty

Poem by: M.G. Wadley

She turns blue while the stars brush the hairs of the moon. Her smile shines through the mouth of the sun, and the hairs upon her arm cuddles upon my chest when we hug. Jewels and gems, everything just to receive nothing, smiles and hearts but still she loves another.

It pours it falls, rain, rain, rain cats and dogs, sniffles, kiffles, bamboo and oats, olive branches and peaches, apples of pine, lemon and lime, oh God her beauty why can't she be mine.

You're the God in goddess, you're the mother of earth, you're my queen that I would confront war within a tabernacle, you're my tabernacle of faith. My lady please let me feel your love, let us make love tonight, please leave that guy alone, he's no good for you.

Broken hearted and confused, tossed aside like Thursdays leftovers, unknown and unsure, waiting to quit but afraid to leave, why do you stay, looking through the crystal ball as she suffers the love of rejection, oh sunflower, oh star please let me plead your case, leave that guy alone.

Blood and misery, tired eyes and her heart is in cased within razors and thorns. Never physically abused, but the verbal abuse is like the marble floor when it is polished.

Again, again, and gain now sapphires and gems, cotton and silk, butter with bread, my queen, my queen, why do you continue to put up with this man. I've been waiting way too long for your acknowledgment. Way too long to sign the deal, way too long for you to drop this scum bag to his depth of insecurity.

Morning has come and you still come to work on foot even in the rain or snow, a fiery pit, the ghouls of the night smiles as the moon becomes tiresome when she clocks into serve.

I cover all her mistakes before she makes them, every conversation she smiles, her eyes and cheeks blushes when she glares upon me, but still as I look on the other side of the glass, I knew what I've done to this lady who loves me, I know I am the monster who mistreated this girl that loves me.

Visualize in Abundance

Chapter 5

The Distance Within

The early mornings and tropical breezes always knocked at my front window on those types of days. I mean I could hear Gospel, R and B, even Hip Hop sometimes on Sundays. The neighborhood and community was just the best place to be before I realized the real components to life. There was so much joy, love and happiness in the spirit of the community. As a child everyday felt like Friday and I use to wish everyday was. Giggles, laughs, games, school, even the crush you have on the boy or girl in class, these were always a major part of my agenda, and I never could wish for more as I was moving into middle school out of elementary. The world to me now was just a pigment of my imagination. The bright lights, the loud hyper sonic music and fresh baking food was the important reality .trend in my life. On the days that it did rain, I use to imagine my life on a sphere, and every moment that I progressed to the next step on my journey, something always hit me hard to the point, that my life took a spin in the right direction. I use to look at the trials of life like a pair of dice, but I was confident to never hit seven. My life up until I graduated from middle school, were considered the glory days. These were the days I knew I would never forget, the dreams that I could always imagine, and the courage to plant my feet and sketch my dreams.

My first year of high school was one of my favorite experiences on my journey so far. I started to understand what it was to have a real friend. I started to learn the purpose of making my priorities dominant. As I continue through school, the glory days started to become a shadow, and the love started to fade. My mind was in a whirlwind, and my heart and emotions were racing to success. It was hard to make decisions about life, and adult decisions when I didn't experience and have the right insight about the different struggles to life.

As I observed the pros and cons of the world around me, it seems as though the atmosphere got colder and I started to see the temptation of lust and envy prosper. I wanted to bring the love back to people hearts. I wanted to break the bridge of hate and dishonor, then reconstruct the barrier of love. Even until this day my life as my own man, and individual has helped me foster my love to be that inspiration of peace. Planting my feet and standing firm, ignited my independence to rehearse my life as a Freedom Hustler. As a Freedom Hustler, it's the burning will of fire that ignites someone self-motivation to bring love and passion back into any individual components of life. Living my life as a Freedom Hustler overall builds discipline in progress and growth, this will open the door to eternal love that will change the course of how love will evolve.

A peak beyond the blind fold

Poem by: M.G. Wadley

What is a cover without the sheet, what is a bed without the comforter, what is a mother without a husband, what is a brother without a sister? What is a piano without the key, what is a door without the lock, what is the right path to follow when there is no road when you look off into the distance?

Take a peak beyond the blind fold, and realize what needs to be seen, realize the grass can be green on both sides, if you grew the right seeds.

Drink enough water so that when the children who starve may taste the liquid from the fountain of youth. Build and build, step and stumble, cry and laugh for I'm a champion so I will prevail.

Break my bones, crush my mind and body, but my spirit lives on. Tie my hands and feet, burn my name from history, and within that same week I will restore the pages to that book. Look down upon me, assassinate my character for the trauma will not last forever.

Fools of the world, ignorance of men and women, respect the craft and not the money, for God does not accept payment beyond the walls. Go ahead and play me, described who I am in the most blasphemous depiction to present any form of life and I will be your greatest icon.

Look past me and count me out, keeping shooting for the stars and not including me in the sequence, for I will be the darkness that you'll have to ask permission to shine.

Ride and drive, speed pass me, accelerate the velocity and you'll see I'm already at the light. The high way is clear with no traffic, with insight

the clouds start to shift together while
the falcon of the middle east skims the
ocean surface on a whim.

<u>Visualize in Abundance</u>

Chapter 6

The Will of Fire

If you love from your heart, that love will never fade. Love is the harmony of passion, and the unbearable emotion to control. Love is the uncontrollable emotion that is a commitment or promise between a love one, also your future lover. In my point of view, you should love with affection and from the heart within, not with the presence of words, and worldly material. Love can be expressed with a hug, the thought of consideration, even just a simple smile. There are five love languages, words, presence, gifts, deeds and the sense of touch. These are the components of love that people use to produce the building block to that level of affection. The words that we use determines not only the view point but the actual decision ignites the connection. The aspects of your ,presence and gifts gives men and women the idea of a long-term relationship, and someone showing that motivation through their trial. In the same manner when young love is fostered overtime, and that love becomes the root of the village that will raise the new generation. The sense of touch and imagery of love are the connection of the deeds we as men and women use to keep the love trend alive.

The deeds lovers produce is the abstract thought of providing the result of a passionate love story that becomes reality. The deed itself is the prosperous action that we as male and female work towards to keep the love we desire afloat. The will of fire is more than just the five languages of love, and the imagery of love itself. The will of fire is the burning sensation of love that lights up the world around it, and drags the hate out of the wilderness into the warmth of a loving heart. A lot of times I allowed the burning flame within my love liquefy like tar and then mantle it on my shoulders as antlers for show. Some days with no money, and nothing to give or offer, majority of the nights you enjoyed with the women you love are forgotten because of the feeling of being ashamed of your appearance. Understanding and realizing that everyone you love or in love with has turned the tables against you and with nothing to offer or provide you just stand silent waiting for your opportunity to walk through.

I use to look at miss butter worth from across the planes and imagine her on the chariot from Gods servants holding palms trees and sunflowers racing across the heavens. Brown butter mocha, I couldn't want for more or desire anything above Cleopatra in the flesh. My Sheba, my queen from the heavens and the place where I thought someone like her didn't exist. I can picture us riding through Jerusalem on a donkey, as she takes hold of the grapes and honey dew, I still act to produce a relaxing massage as I skim the surface of her beauty until no cramp will tempt to re approach her ankles or feet. Letting her know what's real, and how genuine love should be offered, standing as her knight and shining armor listening to her symphonies and cries, I will be determined to cut loose ends with a broken heart. "So, I say unto you, don't allow the fire that burns bright turn into a forest fire just to cancel out, keep and bring forth the love that no one else has to offer."

Stems of Anastasia

Poem by: M.G. Wadley

Cherry red bronze and orange coral trims of the forest bark that seals the stems of Anastasia, the golden goose hatches new life as new life Is birthed and found. Miles away with no one to turn too in the hour of need, the people you once loved, is cast away into a bottle that's sealed away for generations, but new love arises.

The trail awaits and the children of the first men guides the way to a better life, through the essence of pollen that floats. Cherry red blossoms of the afternoon blooms, yesterday morning I moved onto a new tune.

Castles of bubble gum and crisp, mustard linen and cotton loafs of butter, plenty to spread when there's no other. No other way, when there is no way out, follow the stems of

Anastasia follow the dream of contagion.

The red rose is still bright even in the night, the colors alum on the surface of the moon when there's nobody to witness the tune that walks.

We roll and curve, we look to see, we take to have, we believe to be, so why deceive, why deceive when deceit is deception of oneself.

I can see yup I can see, I can see the freedom that's meant to be, fruitful days of the life that I truly see, painted pictures of water color and ink, stencils from heaven condensed, see the picture that's painted. Blue raspberry gems and diamonds from the monsters of the sea, the ship crashes but one life flea, makes it out to spread the word you see, but the truth trips and the carrier creeps in the night with the killer kilt.

Red ruby bronze, milk from the stars, skim the stems of Anastasia so the journey you perceive will be the way beyond the trees, beyond the locust, beyond the leaves, pass the evil where murders believe in the essence of death and the fallen will never rise until the red glow scorches over the topless barrel.

Conceal the case that holds the hearts of the women from the seven springs, allow them to wash the blood from the palms of the hands that takes and devours. Believe in the Cherry blossom that blooms in the night for it will never lose its glow. The light will always stay lit, high lights or low the orange coral trim is the topping on top in same cup when the syrup is split onto a banana.

Follow the Stems of Anastasia for the journey home will not be as comfortable or easy, by pass the sticks

and stones, by pass the walls of
cement for the path divides in
between. The shining door that's two
doors in front beyond a door that
you've been dreaming of, in a place of
no name.

Step beyond the Stems of Anastasia,
close your eyes to the vibe of where
you stand, when the light flashes open
them, and see what you see.

Do you see golden jelly as smooth as

boiling butter and biscuit baked

shelves of knowledge and gold, Riches

beyond belief? Coins of sparkles from

graves of kings and emperors, lost

treasures of children that seek

knowledge in the outer realms on dials

of the ancients. I close the door behind me and I open the lids of my vision, and what do I see.

Cherry red butter bronze stencils and pencils, the coral trim of the pen and pad, with the sparkling light that stares at me face to face to write the perfect script. One red chair an open window, the wind gushes through, the air taps the table of where knowledge forms and stands.

The ink drizzles, as tears runs down the blue lines of the loose leaf, the light stays lit until the switch is off and the

Stems of Anastasia has been watered

and steamed.

<u>*Visualize in Abundance*</u>

Chapter 7

The Roots and Pillars

People tend to say history tends to repeat itself, but without history how can someone learn how to survive and live. There are some people of the world who doesn't understand the significance of other cultures and history. Those who haven't done their homework are foreign to the fact that traditions, cultural beliefs, current events today are from past historic events that lies within our roots. Most occasions that occurred in the past are now life lessons, and references to people who are struggling internally and externally among society. In these references, there are clues and answers for us to reach for higher power and knowledge, so that we may understand the significance of life. I believe we should celebrate and rejoice, about our heritage and ancestry to make us stronger within our minds. As a community and nation, we can honor those who had passed down their love and knowledge to us, then pass that blessing on to our children and the next generation. These blessing will become the legacy of the child who looks like you and me. The boy or girl whose hunger for life is dominant more than a poor man's meal. The growing root that helps the leaf sprout are balanced on pillars. The new generation are the fresh pillars of that leaf, and as a seed of that pillar we cannot let it crumble.

As I sit here and brainstorm about how I don't embrace my culture and heritage enough, the stories and narratives will become foreign to the ears of babes. I have enough trust in myself to become my own apostle for my people and speak for the people who does not want honor the puddles of blood, broken bone and those that are scarred for life. The swamps and trails to freedom for my ancestors endured will always leave a whip lash upon my back, I refuse to forget and ignore how the world revolved around power and misery. Placed in shackles like cattle, stripped of their identity and humanity watched as their daughters were raped and tossed aside, their sons life taken away in the foggy mist of the night. Manifesting the dream of the life I live now, and freedom is on the other side of the field. So how can I forget about them, how can I flee their persecution, I don't even have a strong enough gut to turn down the spirits that continue to latch on to my conscious.

As a man of honor and respect I can't allow my roots to dry out, and the legacy of the unspoken words become silenced. history is not just information or references history tells a story, these recordings and legendary epics tells a story of up rises and down falls, but the most important aspect is my blood and heritage tells me who I am. "So, I say unto you become that shining star and acknowledge the root of the past, become a part of that pillar that holds the leaf so that it may one day grow into a tree. As that tree that stands tall, continue to seek the royalty in the truth and you will be acknowledged as that shining star."

Blood on the sneaks

Poem by: M.G. Wadley

The dirt is dirt less, as the rubble rubs
between my toes through the rubble of
my sneaks. These scuffs and patches,
blue lights and matches, multiple
runs, dodging the heat but holding the
gun. In between the sleep, in between
a ton, in between the cracks as we
come, we come to stir the rum as blood
boils numb.

The walls close in as killers peep, the
eyes that gazes when momma weeps,
do you see the souls of those who chose
this, dark conscious and kings as the
reaper sweeps. Confines and thrashes,
the cold so bare, my breath turns to
ashes. Stains of blood trail the mud,
can a man really be dumber than
dumb, not the actual term but the
decision to fight, to win to learn. The
line runs from the arm to my feet, I
struggle to stand as my vision deplete.
The passage continues to become

shallow as hallow grounds on the Horizon. Crows from every tree top stares in the night, as I lose breath I can't stand the rest, from the face I see, I can't believe the test. Tripping over pebbles and stones, as the new life rises, murder inspires. I trip over pebbles and stones, lanes of quick sand and bones, surfaces of aqua blue puddles, the black cat of the night crawls between my strife and life, the lightening grumbles as the fallen and angels rattle the cages of heavens war room. As I lay, the bay becomes orange from the arising sun, not the beach from this hell whole of a walk way, but I can still smell the rum that drizzled from his bottom lip as the smell diffuses among the muses that sings the song of sorrow for tomorrow morning.

Visualize in Abundance

Chapter 8

Poetry and the sweet sound of Music

Poetry from my point of view is expressing internal emotions, and feelings someone connects to life. Poetry is a component of writing to demonstrate the imagery of love, happiness, and even the darkest thoughts that surrounds you. Poetry is like writing a rap or song to celebrate or narrate a story, event, place or person. Poetry and music are like brother and sister, they're related just much as sleep is the cousin to death, and they relate to connect. Music can be expressed negative or positive but .

most music is an individual's spark of motivation and ambition. Most music in the world helps people among society in good and bad terms but still has a different impact in varied perspectives. As I testify to the wonderful works of ambitious sound, music has always been a positive sensation on the everyday basis in my experience. I snatch out the motivation and glue it to my ambition, there goes my spark into the adventure ahead. Poetry and music can help through hard situations and becomes a stepping stone in good. "So, I say unto you, ask yourself if you inspire and set yourself as an example for others, do you believe you can be that sense of ambition, do you believe you can be that spark of motivation and become that future inspiration. Share your story and let someone else hear the roar of your ambition. Record your trials and legacy so that it may benefit the next child, because it's up to you to share that poem and hear the sweet sound of music."

Puzzles and Pieces

Poem by: M.G. Wadley

The winter blows steam while

the moon smiles green

run young champion run for
the

kingdom you desire

has sprung

sprouted and rooted.

Run young champion run,

run past the cross roads

that intersects and devours the
weak,

run young champion run

chase the highest values,

take it and become meek.

Walls and barriers,

knock, knock they fall

stone and stainless steel

we overcome them all, no man
no women

trespasses beyond this wall. Sparrows,
vultures inherit and slumber for God
see those who prays from under.

whistle and tweet

for the angels of heaven has kneeled
and believed.

Visualize in Abundance

Chapter 9

A goal to reach

Pushing forward, and having confidence is always a positive way of life. Confidence is the central trait that's equivalent to faith, hope, and determination. These components of life are tools to use to absorb more knowledge, and to walk a brighter path, and to achieve a higher goal. Life passes like a speeding bullet, with no name, no answers and no guarantees. Consider your future is only an idea and expression of any life pursuers self-desire. A goal should be a bolt in anybody life who wishes to progress in success. Goals are reaching points in comparison to success. These utilities are the spark of dedication towards a successful ending. A goal is like a shooting star, it shines so bright that you crave the success, .but it takes a dedicated achiever to reach it.

Stones and Gems

Poem by: M.G. Wadley

Seven summers has pass for
new winters arrive within a
sunset spring. 1080 Seasons
revolve, revolves around the
horizon of Jupiter, descending
among the tunnel commanding
the lapsed soul, the fallen has
risen.

The clouded judgement married into
despair, while the lily of the modest
rose diffuses a new stem. Born into the
lamp of the crystal ball where they all
fall into pieces.

Wonders of wonderful delights that
conquer humanity overnight. yet he
who stands before the lambs of
Babylon and the lions of the most high

delivers his people from oppression and misery.

Pearls of me and pearls of you, she shines in the east on the other side of west, when the blood moon rises on the horizon of rubies as ashes pray.

Linen and gems, stones of blood concealed within what's already of ten. Hot steams grave the stone of the merchants who sells purity. who else cries out in the middle of the night, where thieves and robbers lurk, patiently wait for the light of what's bright, step into, unto and become.

Visualize in Abundance

Chapter 10

Distinguished beyond belief

All knowledge is always powerful knowledge. Education, ambition, and your will of fire distinguishes people from one another not to say you're better than another person, but to acknowledge your skills and achievements as your own individual. In my opinion every male and female should use their knowledge to build, construct and create a better world. To create a world of our deepest dreams, we must make a change to ourselves.

Realize the bad habits you conduct, pull out the cancer that disrupts the flow of life within you and subside the quitter that wants to shine. Connect to one another, and share a bond of love and peace, as time spins forward you will have happiness. The ability you have, is the important aspect to life that gives you the opportunity to inspire the new generation. Any boy or girl can be distinguished during their academic experience, or just their simple hunger for life.

Being distinguished through my eyes is the one or two people in class that are considered the eye ball among the bunch, the people who sit by themselves that are considered weird, these are the ones who will be the most distinguished beyond your belief. The fabric of their clothing and the actions of society does not manifest within their true character or conclude their future. The one who walks alone, is not insecure or scared of the world around him or her bounds, but the intuition of their independence is the flame that the water flows between their teeth as they speak life from the belly. The one girl who doesn't have the pretty features or the popular trend that's considered worthy becomes worthless in the eyes of those who follow the world from the faces within the next seat. The boy who doesn't view the world as his brothers becomes an outcast in same manner when there's only a small number of even and more odds in one room. The belief in oneself is the faith that will keep the promise from turning too far on a broken knob, as the wheel spins forever in your favor. There will be people who will change the perception of a face that's unfamiliar in their world, the one face that you once knew is now questioned by your judgment from false assumptions and personal fault, do not become a wounded animal when you can avoid slaughter and mischief, stay distinguished in your own world. Remember your world, stay within reality but create a picture that will last forever, even as you crop and trim the puzzles will never scatter if you keep them intact, stay distinguished.

White fox's
Of the color wheel

Poem by: M.G. Wadley

Mama always told me to forget about the life beyond the woods, but I never understood her fears. Mama always told me baby girl life doesn't ride the sunset on a color wheel, to enter Gods kingdom, let the kingdom be within.

Children of the land children of the poor, children of the riches you come and search for more, Sit and feast for the scribes will tell the tales of the white fox's.

Guess and think, doubt or believe for this no folklore just think and believe. The young girl who sees the flow of the color wheel will become the merchant of heaven, but her ties will bound her to the surface.

As the night turned into light, and rivers rebirth new life, the butterflies of the meadow engages into whistles of the wind. Waters clear as crystal, and the young girl who seeks the world beyond the woods wonders the cross roads to freedom.

Overnight she returns home to an abandoned cabin with no lights or food to feast. Dust and empty cabinets no sign of life, no sign of all the voices she's use too screaming from the rear door.

As the rain drops from the sky and the thunder roars across the land, no animal will ever understand when the moon cries.

Boom, boom, pitch, splash, father mother where have you gone, where are you, where are your father because I need your protection. Mother, mother why won't you respond, why do you ignore my cries, just why. All the doors slam and the whistles of the wind whispers in her ears as she falls to the depth of darkness, she awakens and the animals of the regions gathers from all corners of the earth.

Sing and dance of the wild, bring forth the Eagle of the valley, bring forth the Bambi of every child memoir in their animated pursuit.

The delicate flower arose and the forest kneeled before her, the birds kneeled before her, the lions kneeled before her as the fairies danced upon her shadow as she stands firm with a glare.

A bright light shines between her eyes and feet, there and there, look over there, no too your right, look there, there they surround with glossy silver eyes of the stars, fur white as the snow from the sky above.

Twelve fox's total, the same twelve that guided me in my dreams beyond the clouds, I stood light as a feather, I could see the motion of Hawks peak, as it soars the horizon. As I ride its back, the dolphins leap from the tropical waters into the clouds we glide through.

Creatures never before seen follows my trail. All the insects of the land swirls into the suns pupil, Butterflies springs from their hold and the nest that's left behind become the resurrection of the phoenix. As I jumped down into the colors of the wind, the tree of life is off into a distant descript, standing tall above all the land and the clouds the moon smiles and kneels before my footsteps upon the mountain.

Rumble and grumble, six of the white fox's appear before her with gifts of food, guided to the lake to drink with the unknown of the sea.

Creatures with the head of a vulture, the body of a sphinx and the tail of a donkey. Creatures with faces of lost spirits which become the unknown.

Toss and turn shout and praise the young girl who will sit on the throne, the loving daffodil, the angel on the moon. Mother Lilith you have returned.

She moves forward in a realm she feels familiar too, foreign to the parts she roams as she look for the answers she continually seek.

She continues to head in the direction the white fox's guide her, first there were six, now there are eight, no ten. Anywhere I look or turn, one of them is there to serve or protect. Across the grasslands, across the kingdoms of the stars. No matter where the fox's guide me, I can still see the tree of life.

Angels of millions soar the sky, black on black Crows confused and mild, bring forth the mother of the first, bring forth the women who denies his hand.

Compassionate and merciful, loving and forgiving, almighty creator, who am I, who am I father, no answers of discussion just silence.

Blooms of ruins, ruby red jewels, sapphire of dust lanes, honey gold grain, this is never before seen, if you have never entered into the lighted tunnel. She finally arrives, she's finally here, the mother of life will finally appear, sheets of flower, the air filled with pineapples and oranges, strawberries and cream, raisins and oats, with owls on every tree.

Beautiful children sing and greet, as I enter the kingdom within the life of trees, tulips blossom and birds sing as I approach the throne of the king of kings.

My king, king my king, I do not want to leave this place for everything is happiness, please my grace, keep me among thee.

So, bright too light for Mans eye to see, are you God, are you the one from my seven dreams, and as the *silhouette turns around, two white fox's crystal clean.*

I awake from my slumber within my dreams, I still look up towards the sky a rainbow appears within colors eye. The sun so bright within the miles, wheels of color, blinds the clouds.

Distance within the color wheel.

Visualize in Abundance

Chapter 11

Religious pursuit

Reaching out to grab gods hand, and accepting the blessings of the golden fruit that shines in the dark itself will be the glass road that will lead you beyond the golden gate. The lessons that you learn are the blessings of God love that will walk with you forever as you progress with faith on your journey. The hope, the idea that sits in the back of your head, and you start to wonder about the right path to follow. As you adapt to the shallow voice you start to respond to the voice for the answers, the momentum of your struggles continues to increase and the ladder to success becomes possible. As I look beyond the glass window, the lights of God eye open the heavens upon the surface of the earth and my spirit is drifted away. My body is afloat beyond the clouds, and my eyes are my tunnel for vision. Beautiful faces accompany me along the ride to the golden gate as I arrive to greet my Lord. The thought, the very passion at that instant moment of beauty and divinity, my world is on the tip of the mountain and I stand on its highest peak. As I close my eyes to see the truth of what's soon to come, my faith in God, and curiosity to sit at Jesus table has become, one of my moral ambitions to pursue Gods passion. The vision that I seek is the sight that I witness. I hear nothing but

the streams of water that runs like a
waterfall, golden as the purest honey
that any man has stumbled upon the
surface of the earth. Temples that
reflects the face of the sun, the echo of
the kingdoms ahead, but still my
words are silent as my spirit walks
among the city of the father.
Continuing to wonder in faith as my
knowledge of God literacy boils my
blood to see and prosper the full truth.
Falling in love with the footsteps of
Jesus, and allowing my enlightenment
to sprout and diffuse among my peers.
Gods revelation and the epic of the
apostles has become the tangerine in
my spiritual memoir of the father and
son bond of one. Beauty and
magnificent beasts roam the heavens,
and watch the earth as man and

women become pigments of sin. I encourage you to allow the creatures of divinity to enlighten the realms of darkness that is fostered deep within your heart. Grab Gods hand and accept the honey dew that is sprung from the tree of life, make it your backbone. Believe in Jesus Christ, as I would tell any individual regardless if its within my community, a close friend, my brother and sister even the man who despise the very belief I stand behind. Pray for your heart to be like his, imitate his image, seek his story and love. Rejoice in his name and be proud to know that you're in his picture, believe that when he looks down the end of the table, God will have a glimpse of your face.

I couldn't picture Gods face and appearance, I can't even grasp the idea of angels and power beyond my comprehension. As I sit and think, what if I could pray to God so hard that he will descend upon a cloud of lightening with angels scouting between every cloud. Standing firm while I witness the glory of God offer his hand, my arms reach out, but my feet are planted stone. The brightest white blinds my sight, my sins are radiated from the pores of my skin and here I wake. Everything in my room still in place, its beautiful outside, Gods eye is shining bright and the pigeons are the doves I have been chasing my entire life. Everything is silent and the spirits of the universe dances beside me as I travel to see my lord. With no one around and the silence of the wind twinkles the dust of Gods kingdom upon the crown of my head. Gabriel swindles by me, the trumpets of salvation surround the tunnel of my beliefs, while Jesus breaks the chains of condemnation, changes all the locks that temptation has access to prevail. The night has come, the minions of the lake of fire are in full awareness of their purpose. Craving and soaking in the blood of the innocent, devouring the lost souls who lost direction on Jacobs ladder. The devil dances as he intercepts the faith of Gods children, snatching the children from the arms of their mother, using the love from within a family bond as a decoy to pursue his true intentions. Look within the eyes of a man, look through the thrush hole of his soul, acknowledge the chariots of the champions who fight for a righteous heart. Pay close attention to the flying cars as you cross the street, observe the direction the birds and trees bend and twirl as the reaper sweeps through the streets you call home. The angel of death is just at the next corner, what will you do when you come face to face with death. What will you do if you're on the opposite side of the gun, your life can be taken away in the blink of an eye, so I advise you not to become the interception. Your mind and body are one, we are created in Gods image, we are his temples, we are his children. I can vision the grass plains, I can vision the son of God speaking the parables of his father, as I stand there and observe my lord bless the people of his image. Spread the loaf, share the blood of his sacrifice, teach the children about the greatest teacher who ever walked the face of the earth, expose the footsteps of his ministry, chase the shadow of Jesus. I'm not here to persuade anyone to convert their religion, but I am here to share my testimonies of God grace and blessings. "So, I say unto you, believe in whatever your spiritual intuition magnifies for your goal in open up within any vital spot, believe in his sacrifice and love, believe in his miracles and parables, soak in his way of life, seek the tree of life and there you will see him."

Phoenix Flower Sun

Poem by: M.G. Wadley

As I surface among the branches
of the forest, I continue to search for a
way out. It's only a glimpse of
freedom is just on the other side of the
river, dogs chase after my scent and
my body grows tiresome as the sun
rays compels the lashes and chains
that has scarred me for life. The dirt
continues to endorse the thorns that
tear away the flesh I condone between
the mount in the hills. Just a few steps,
just a few more the way to another
way between the wolfs howl and the
hawks peak. I find myself along the

rivers path and now I come to rest between the branches.

The sun is hot and I smell food and spices that I never sniffed before, lights that expand the surrounding between the trees that carries me within a distance. As I walk in circles, this cloud of mist engulfs the air that tugs at my throats voice when the cycle of dust disperses. Flames await the yellow residue lingers along the trail that follows me to freedom, heart beating to a burst and the pupils of my eyes print the path to that path of a new life.

The vines of the roots build the contagion of blood that flows from the heart of life out of the abyss, they come and lurk they lurk, to the tallest mount, hovering breath over logs and nuggets of rice that compels the butter from ball that's curved. I'm there I'm here, oh god I'm here, horns blow while bells rings, my heart sings while my spirit makes it on board but my body bares the pain. The light gets dim and tears press against the bone of my cheek, I guess no one will ever know.

Visualize in Abundance

Chapter 12

The New Nativity

Every individual knows their own ability and skill at a certain age when they decide to work towards their dreams. The next step and new door that opens creates the experience that ignites the new adventure. From my own insight, the best adventure to live is the experience of your up rises and down falls which creates the experience of a life time. Developing on your journey is your personal acceptance letter and commitment to the goals you want to achieve. Considering the imagery of your goals might be the truth of your drive, part of that hunger that you will crave may be the result of passionate struggles you must endure. The struggles in life is what balance the concept of negative and positive and it provides the mechanical parts that will lead you beyond the ladder of success. As time moves forward, you must vision your future, you must see the dreams and goals you've always desired. The new adventure awaits anyone who is willing to come face to face with defeat itself, the pain, the lost hope, the doubting thought and temptation to lead you astray.

Have a focus and keep it consistent, save that one child who doesn't have the legs to walk in blind faith, save the child who eyes has no vision and ears are concealed shut. Save the little girl who cries out when she's in despair, comfort her and make her feel protected. Influence her intellect to be a lady, discard the bribes and trickery that proclaims the lust of the world. Break the cycle of not honoring the heritage of family, how is a man a man when he doesn't see the significance of the blood that flows in his veins. How will the young boy who only see death and murder in his path put down the gun. His future and existence has become a maybe and his tears will never flow because of his loyalty to the streets. Angry to the world, feels like everyone owes him an answer, but the wait for a response becomes a drastic hold.

Believing nothing will stop him, he takes the stakes into his own hands, rolls the dice and within due time his life spans runs out. There goes another soul, another loss spirit who didn't serve his purpose. "So, I say unto you grab his hand before he pulls the trigger, close his mouth before the devil creeps out, keep him on the same pavement that your feet walk among. Keep his mind in the loop of fantasies, and love. Introduce to him another way to be successful, keep our brothers and sister's spirits as a child. Man, or woman, it's our priority to make an inclusion about the terms we instruct and practice, bring forth the lamb of God so that the little children we raise may drink of the same bowl, breathe in the air that the holy son has provided to prevail against all odds." Sacrifice anything that is meaningless, anything that is worthless or unbeneficial discard of it, dismember all loose screws and break down any door that stands firm, remove it from the hinges and put it into the hands of the next man. Bind the feet of anyone or anything that intends to trample over the losses and defeats that you endured. Show disbelievers the truth behind the gallant trophy, show the world you're the one willing to go beyond mountains, prove it to yourself that you're the Hercules of your nativity. A child only Follows and pursue what they believe is the righteous path to follow, I look upon the kids who roam free of love in the dessert of hate and sorrow as they find comfort on the shallow rock we call the corner.

A man who poisons children, dilutes their mind with the potions of the inferno, a man who would sharpen the dagger of weapon to rise against any boy or girl salutes them into the fire to burn of sin and evil deeds that's cast into the soil that sprouts. The stone road becomes wasted, as the cold air grips the dust from the bottom of each foot step That's taken on the way of a new lane that's created for success.

Bronze Feet and wool hair

Poem by: M.G. Wadley

Beyond the desserts and
behind the

Trees

I preach I preach within the seven
leaves

Seasons come and
seasons go

reflect the water

on the oceans

coast.

Holy, holy I am the ghost

Father and son nothing to boast

But I preach the word
I am the host.
Come children come and eat the
Bread
See the truth as you lay to bed
Now I depart into another land
Oceans and water
In the palm of hand.
Death and murder, whips and bands
The rooster croaks within
my span
but I still love them all.

The road is long the
story awaits
The followers come but one deflates
Crowds and rumors,
Famous within the states.

Witness the miracles as haters hate
those of God still debate.

How much how much do you need to
see

That the kingdom of God

sits feet to
feet.

Eat and feast

Sing and dance for the time will come
when I

Rise again.

Visualize in Abundance

Chapter 13

The Memoir Blossom

It appears as though the world to me was the repetition sequence of an author's poetic love story, and a hero's victory in their most difficult battle or challenge in life. I could feel the nature of the world grab onto my hair, as if it was physical enough to touch me. Anywhere I walked or traveled it seemed the sunlight from God eye always shined upon me, and I was lifted from all my guilt and sorrow. The way I viewed the trees, the reaction of civilization, the decisions among society, the very air I breathed was the memory of the lost and the rainy days were the tears of a clown who could not smile or laugh. I felt like I could become someone's inspiration I feel like I could be the love of my life champion. I wanted the kids who looks like me believe a dream, dream could be achieved more than they can see with the naked eye. My dreams didn't revolve around the riches, and the value of a dollar. I only want someone to see life through and African American male who lives in the slums of North Philadelphia, and dreams bigger than a Christian preacher believing to enter the gates of heaven. Moving passed the taunts of the streets, denying the badge from the bottom of the barrel, making my decisions crucial and careful. Hell, on earth, and it has reigned over the weak and vulnerable, I have felt pain and I experienced victory. Looking through my eyes, the eyes of a winner, the eyes of a champion, and the eyes of a servant of God. It feels good to know about prayers that goes up and comes down, so I say unto you, keep God as your blessing. I feel like I can map my life out and balance it on a scale, lay it out on the world map and declare it's mine. My name and stamp on each state and country, my laughter and enthusiasm is played on the Cassette tape while the air conditioner cools you down on a hot summer day. I had some hard hits and staying above float almost seemed impossible. I could see the climax, so far away out in the distance but the resolution was a mystery. Michael Jackson, James brown or even the sound of Jim Croce that creates the melody of soul sparked my drive and it

made me feel invincible, I still salute to
Marvin and Smokey it gave my
confidence and ambition the relation to
always move forward with love. Surfing
along the dotted line, understanding the
tales of time and how the sages of the
future never stop ticking. Your hair
starts to grow old, feet continuing to
hurt your fantasies drift off into the
sunset. Each day I woke up felt like I
created a new tune and new sound to
my life, but I surely did feel the rhythm
and beat as I continued to progress in
my life's journey.

The memories of any man or
woman is what creates the memoir of
the adventure, the failure and pain
ignites the spark of determination. The
determination inside oneself inner spirit
will always move into the light and

vanishes out of the darkness. The trials and struggles people face shapes the blossom that blooms twice. Each day creates a new opportunity for my journey, and it opens the gates to a new story. Waltz with your competition, inform them of the capsules you had to release to win, let the bruises heal the time you value precious. You can get an idea of my life like a yellow lotus flower that shines bright in the dark. The evil of this world continues to try and triumph over my happiness, the taunts and temptation that seeks to skirmish my existence. Who am I, I am the black hero that will stand up as a soldier for the people who were scourge by the trials of life. I am the poor boy who sits on the throne and pulls up the neighborhood bum from starvation, splits the butter and bread with anyone who has a rumbling stomach. Who am I, I am the man who is willing to give a gallon just to receive a cup, betrayed and deceived, but still forgives. Who am I, I am the son of a true Queen, a woman with the ambition of a man but has the heart brighter than the whitest lily in any valley. Raised and groomed by the fruits of the Gods, I'm thankful for Ambrosia I'm blessed to have my Aunt Angie. Elevating in the love of my mother, carrying the blood line from the trenches to a utopia of myths. Riding along the tune that gets my heart pumping, releasing the poetic lavishness from the royalties that I call jewels. The sapphire and gems shine bright as you smile, sharpen the stones that you collect, build your drive with the same bricks you collected as stone. Cast your stone out into the sea, and watch the pebbles wash ashore, look closely at the pebbles, pay close attention to the pearls that lay between your toes. The numbers of pearls are too great to account for, these will be the descendants of your legacy and trophies. This is my perspective and this is my story to tell. Maybe one day I will inspire that boy or girl, maybe one day I will become that champion that's written in history. This is my life, my test and my results. Become that shining star and become that blossom that blooms twice, the new generation, the hunger and trials are essential to the person you become in life. Reach out into the world with all heart with the bounds of belief and faith, let God guide you, become the vessel of his body and mind. Keep the will of fire torched, insure the flame never goes out, and success will delight you with open arms as you become that inspiration in history.

A place with no name

Poem by: M.G. Wadley

The tea pot stays hot from the
burns of the metal blend of ember. The
steam rolls into the dust that deflates
the minerals of what's around us into
despair. As the souls pass through the
realm of life and death, the reapers of
the shallow halls come to collect. The
tea pot stays hot from the burns of the
metal blend of ember. Towers of glass
and grass crystal creeks, can you see
the divine tree. Sparkles of eclipses
and black holes, the stars fall to the
surface of the earth and new birth
conceals the tea pot that stays hot
from the ember fire blend.

Fire from the dirt, murder of its worth, the lust of the homicidal curse is glorified by those of oppression. Dragged through the mud and trenches, the heart beat panics as death glances beyond the eye.

Bundles and rolls of silver, yellow tape of ink to record the greatest story ever told. Lights of aqua blue, bronze butter gold smooth as royal silk when the inferno arise.

<u>Visualize in Abundance</u>

Colors of the wind

Poem by: M.G. Wadley

The rain pours for Jerome as the heavens cry for the loss of a child of God. The rain pours for Jerome as the heavens cry for the loss, of a child of God, for he dances in the meadow with the lost souls of Eden. The rain pours for Jerome, for today is the day life was born, within the colors of the wind. A dove scuffs pass the corner of my eye, and whispers Daughtry has made it to the promise land. The rain pours on this sunny day where bright lights take within the distance of Novembers leaf. Pains and sorrow reach to grab me in the dark alley where killers call home. One arm pulls me forward for I know the hands of this man. The metal pole is still firm and standing in a place where I lost a good friend, someone smiles and waves across from that cold alleyway.

*I know for sure, I know that smile,
that face is too familiar. One last
glance as I look behind me as the rain
drops, Jerome floats away with the
colors of the wind and his voice still
lingers around that street light.*

Sunrise Nov 29th 1992   Sunset July 22nd 2013

<u>*Visualize in Abundance*</u>

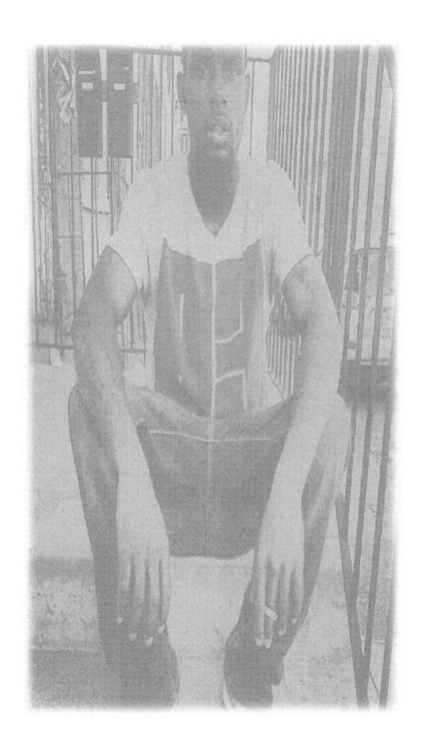

Made in the USA
Middletown, DE
05 July 2020

11764983R00084